MOUTHFUL

AF005840

MATT STARR

DREAM BABY PRESS

A DREAM BABY PRESS BOOK

Select poems from *MOUTHFUL* first appeared in *The New Yorker*, *Interview Magazine* and *Far West Press*.

This book is a work of fiction. Names, characters, places and incidents are either the product of the author's imagination or are used fictitiously. Any resemblance to actual persons, living or dead, events or locales is entirely coincidental.

All rights reserved. No part of this book may be reproduced in whole or in part without written permission from the publisher, except by reviewers who may quote brief excerpts in connection with a review in a newspaper, magazine, or electronic publication; nor may any part of this book be reproduced, stored in a retrieval system, or transmitted in any form or by any means electronic, mechanical, photocopying, recording, or other, without written permission from the publisher.

Edited by Elinor Hitt
Cover Design by Matt Starr, Zack Roif, Jess Kuronen, and Julia Muell

ISBN: 979-8-9898406-0-1

Copyright © 2024 by Matt Starr
All Rights Reserved
Printed in the United States of America
July 2024
First Edition

For Mom, Dad, Adam, and Mackenzie

TABLE OF CONTENTS

- 9   Adult Supervision
- 11   Family Bonding
- 12   Self-Portrait
- 15   I Am Paddington Bear
- 16   Everything a Girl I Like Stole From CVS in Her Twenties
- 17   Am I Special?
- 18   East Village, 4th Street
- 20   Life or Death
- 21   Macaroni and Cheese
- 22   Jealousy
- 23   Lifestyles of the Rich and Famous
- 24   Under the Sea
- 25   The Unbearable Lightness of Being Me
- 26   The Library
- 28   Advice for Young Boys
- 30   Mouthful
- 31   Most Kids

32	Mouth to Mouth
33	Comfortably Numb
34	Everything a Girl I Like Licked as a Kid
35	Check Up
36	Law of Attraction
37	Heat Stroke
38	Grandma
39	Living
40	Every Medication Taken by a Girl I Like in Her Twenties
41	Dessert
42	Around the World
43	Sunday Afternoon
44	Bathroom Trash
45	Nighttime
46	Distractions
47	Slushy
48	Titles of Gay Porn Videos I Found in the West Village at 5am

50	Home on the Range
52	Everything a Girl I Like Did in Bed at Twenty-Three
53	Pink
54	Marge
56	The Super Man
57	Masters of the Universe
58	Mom
59	Off Course
60	A River Runs Through It
63	True Love
64	Getting Spanked at Target
65	Life Cycle
68	Galaxy Quest

ADULT SUPERVISION

growing up
my brother and i
would take our dad's
power drill
and stick hot dogs
on the end of it

we'd turn it
to the lowest setting
and try sucking them off
while they spun around
in circles

we would tease each other
pulling the drill
in and out
of our mouths

we'd bob at them
like fish
reaching for flies

sometimes
we'd tie each other's hands up
and hold our mouths open wide
slowly moving the drill
closer and closer
until it was all the way in

and see how long
we could hold it for
before attempting
to suck the hot dog off
the drill bit

it was always easier
on our knees

we did this for a year
until our parents
walked in on us
and told us
we couldn't play
with power tools anymore
without adult supervision

but because our parents
worked so late
we never had them around
to supervise us
so we never did it again

and now
they don't buy us
hot dogs anymore

FAMILY BONDING

mom and i were both
diagnosed with depression

we weren't rich
and only one of us
had health insurance

so she got
a doctor's prescription
and we split the bottle

and now
we are both
a little
happier

SELF-PORTRAIT

i hated drawing
as a kid

everyone called me
retarded

i really only liked
to draw
Bambi with boobs

one time i tried
drawing a self-portrait
but it just turned out
looking like
Bambi with boobs

so maybe
they were right

I AM PADDINGTON BEAR

i am a tiny
brown bear
named Paddington
and i like men

i'm not sure
if that comes across
in my movies or not
it probably doesn't
not my fault

believe me
i've tried very hard
to make my movies
more gay

i've had horrible arguments
with the writers
and producers about it

i've asked for outfit changes
to fall in love
with another male bear
to be just a tad more sophisticated
and they give me nothing

somehow they've taken
a sex positive bear in real life
and usurped his sexuality
and turned him into
a sexless
asexual bear

which couldn't be
further from the truth

on the contrary
i have a very healthy sex life
i've got multiple partners
some casual
others more romantic

i love sex
and i'm not ashamed of it
and neither should my character be

EVERYTHING A GIRL I LIKE STOLE FROM CVS IN HER TWENTIES

Silver nail polish (Essie and Sally Hansen)

45 8.4oz Red Bulls

Nude lipstick

Clear lip gloss

Strawberry and s'mores flavored Pop-Tarts

Acne cream

CeraVe face wash (travel size)

Hair ties

Sewing needles

A 10 pack of ballpoint pens

Allegra allergy medicine (during the summer)

A toothbrush

Pink hair dye

Scissors

Scrunchies

Eyeshadow (that she never used)

Monistat

Composition notebooks

Shampoo

and tweezers

AM I SPECIAL?

i keep telling myself
that i am
but i'm starting
to have my doubts

EAST VILLAGE, 4ᵀᴴ STREET

i live in the East Village
on 4th Street
i'm 13 now

my parents are artists
and they don't care
if i go to school
so i don't

instead
i stay home
watch movies
and order Domino's

i can't get enough of
their Chicken Kickers

after i finish eating
when i'm feeling really full
and good about myself

i strip naked
stand in front of the window
and watch all the people walk by

we live next to
a police station
and when they walk by
i wave
and they stare

i like to turn on the radio
real loud
to 105.9
the classical station
and move my body
slow and gentle
like a flower

i saw this movie
with Patrick Swayze
where he's dancing topless
and that's what i like to think of
when i'm dancing naked
in the window

LIFE OR DEATH

20 pounds overweight
when you're 7
is death

MACARONI AND CHEESE

when we were kids
you pulled down my pants
and i was confused
and cold
then i pulled down yours
and you were confused
and cold
after
we ate
macaroni and cheese
and the thought
of doing anything else
went away

JEALOUSY

the homeless woman
always begging us for food
in front of our
apartment building
has bigger boobs
than my girlfriend

this makes her insecure
and it's all
she talked about for a week

she couldn't believe
someone with no money
bad hygiene
and a terrible sense of fashion
has bigger and better
breasts than her

she said i couldn't
look at her
talk to her
give her food
or else

LIFESTYLES OF THE RICH AND FAMOUS

Bette Davis insured her waist for $28,000

Jimmy Durante insured his nose for $50,000

Dolly Parton insured her boobs for $600,000

Holly Madison insured her boobs for $1,000,000

Rihanna insured her legs for $1,000,000

Keith Richards insured his hands for $1,600,000

Madonna insured her boobs for $2,000,000

Jamie Lee Curtis insured her legs for $2,000,000

Heidi Klum insured her legs for $2,000,000

Tina Turner insured her legs for $3,200,000

Kylie Minogue insured her butt for $5,000,000

Bruce Springsteen insured his vocal chords for $6,000,000

Daniel Craig insured his body for $9,500,000

America Ferrera insured her smile for $10,000,000
(paid for by Aquafresh)

Jennifer Lopez insured her butt for $27,000,000

Julia Roberts insured her smile for $30,000,000

Taylor Swift insured her legs for $40,000,000

Mariah Carey insured her legs for $70,000,000

David Beckham insured his legs for $195,000,000

and i don't have insurance at all
and my weekly unemployment check
is only $159.25
after taxes are taken out

UNDER THE SEA

the best place to get fingered
in the Museum of Natural History
is under the large stairwell
right when you enter the room
with the big blue whale
next to
the northern elephant seal display
next to
a bathroom
that's rarely used

it's dark
romantic
and feels spontaneous

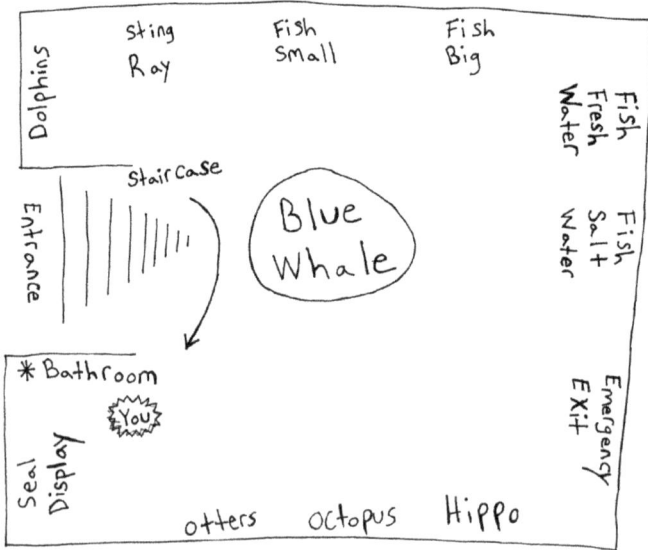

THE UNBEARABLE LIGHTNESS OF BEING ME

your belly button
is my favorite hole
because
it's the one
i can never have

THE LIBRARY

i used to go to
the public library
to watch porn

i wasn't alone

it was me
and all the
homeless people

some of them
would take
pictures of the screen
on their Sprint cell phones
and go to the bathroom

i'd look at
camel toe websites
BangBus.com
and Girls Gone Wild videos

i wouldn't go
to the bathroom
but i would
print out photos
of the girls
and take them home

i loved the blonds
in pink and yellow
g-strings

i loved the girls who said
they were from Midwest schools

that's why i ended up going
to Indiana University

i wanted to meet girls
like the ones
on the bus

they seemed so normal
and innocent
and i loved that

i feel normal and innocent
especially
when i'm looking at porn
in the public library

ADVICE FOR YOUNG BOYS

i was approached
by this little boy
in the park

he was alone
probably 8 or 9

he took off his shirt
and started showing off
his muscles
flexing his biceps
for me

he asked me
to take off my shirt
so he could see
my muscles too

he started
asking questions
about my diet
and what kind of
workouts i did

he told me
that he wished
he had more muscles
in his upper body
and wanted a 6-pack

he said
he loved watching
men's bodies in movies
and wanted his
to look like theirs

i told him
there were things
he could do
to look like that

i showed him
websites like
www.menshealth.com
and www.muscleandfitness.com

but i said
ultimately
the most important thing
he could do
was to just watch
what he ate

he didn't like that though
and he clearly
didn't like being
told what to do

he called me
a faggot
and ran away

MOUTHFUL

in special ed
when Miss Levitt
would leave the room

the six of us
would run around
and try to stick our tongues
down each other's throats

the goal was
to do it with everyone
before Miss Levitt came back

sometimes
she never came back
and we would keep going
until our mouths went dry

a few of the kids
couldn't even speak
but they could definitely kiss

MOST KIDS

most kids
don't know this
or don't think about it
but every time i look
at an adult woman
or anyone over the age of 16
i know they've given
a blow job
like my mom, my sister,
and all my teachers
or when i look
at an adult man
i know they've had
a vagina in their face
like my dad, my rabbi,
and all of my friend's fathers
it's all i see
and it's blinding
most kids
don't think about
this kinda stuff
but i do

MOUTH TO MOUTH

in the shower
i let you take the water
from your mouth
and spit it into my mouth

i like when you have
soap in your eyes
and can't see me
watching you

COMFORTABLY NUMB

fuck me hard
fuck me soft

i don't care
i'm on Zoloft

EVERYTHING A GIRL I LIKE LICKED AS A KID

AAA batteries

A linoleum floor

A cold car window

Nickels

The tips of glue sticks

Hardened Play-Doh

Perfume ads in fashion magazines

The television screen

The remote

Gum from the bottom of her classmate's shoe

A T.J. Maxx gift card

An iPod Shuffle

Computer keyboards

The blades of a handheld fan

Colored construction paper

Her friend Gracie's metal bed frame

Ice cubes

The tips of ballpoint pens

Her best friend's hardwood floors

Scratch and sniff stickers

Her science textbook

The slime from science class

and green and pink paint chips from Home Depot

CHECK UP

the doctor walked in
and asked if i was
sexually active
with males, females, or both

i said females
but wished it were both

LAW OF ATTRACTION

i don't like girls
with nose jobs
which is why it's weird
that i'm attracted to you

i wasn't sure at first
if you had one
but now it's pretty clear

HEAT STROKE

it's 8am
and i lie naked in my bed
like i always do
at this hour

the curtains are open
and i let the sun hit
the crack of my ass

i flex my cheeks
opening and closing them
controlling the amount of rays
that go inside me

the day must begin
but not
until i'm fully charged

GRANDMA

my grandma
was an extra
in the 1971 film
McCabe & Mrs. Miller

she was one of the prostitutes
and had her breasts
played with on screen
for two-and-a-half seconds
while sitting on a guy's lap
an hour into the film

this was the only role
she ever got

LIVING

sometimes words
get stuck in my throat

sometimes lots of things
get stuck in my throat

but that doesn't stop me
from living

EVERY MEDICATION TAKEN BY A GIRL I LIKE IN HER TWENTIES

Concerta

Vyvanse

Focalin

Valium

Ativan

Lexapro

Zoloft

Abilify

Claritin

Zyrtec

Allegra

Ibuprofen

and Tums

DESSERT

i wanna
lick your
fingers
one by one
until i'm full

AROUND THE WORLD

there are 7.7 billion people
currently living on the Earth
one third of them are sexually active
averaging once per week
meaning 370 million people
are having sex each day
and if the average duration of sex
is 7 minutes
and there are 206 sex time slots
in a day
then that means
1.8 million people
are having sex right now

and i'm not one of them

SUNDAY AFTERNOON

i watched her chug
a Red Bull
and pluck out
each individual
pubic hair
one by one

it took over an hour
and she barely
acknowledged
me sitting
next to her

BATHROOM TRASH

gum
wine bottle
coconut water
condom
Pedialyte Pops

NIGHTTIME

candy
movie
shower
bed
mouth
sleep

DISTRACTIONS

a mouthful of
Chick-fil-A
was heaven
to you

a mouthful of me
was just
a distraction

SLUSHY

i didn't know
the joy i'd feel
when i bought you
the lemonade slushy
at the fair today

had i known
this drink
would turn to pee
and end up
in my mouth
i would've
ordered you 2

TITLES OF GAY PORN VIDEOS I FOUND IN THE WEST VILLAGE AT 5AM

MTV's Cute Naked Guy

One Night In A Youth Hostel

Up Your Ass

Little Big League

Comrades In Arms

Playing With Monsters

Call of the Wild

Thick As Thieves

The Vampire of Budapest

Power Boys

Dirty Dreaming

Tender Trick (Santa Monica BLVD)

Viva Ibiza

Going The Distance

An American Man

Billy 2000

Hot Wheels

Rod of Steal

Beach Buns

Tall Tails (Mustang)

Red Alert (Falcon)

Dynastud

Other Side of Aspen

Night Riders

Glory Holes of S.F.

The Bigger They Come

Below The Belt

Manrammer

Just Between Us, You Promise

Men For All Seasons

Shadows In The Night

Pump It Up

Thunder Balls

X Large

Backseat BJ

Below The Decks

Out of Bounds

Winner Takes All

Flavor of Men

Hot Cops (No. 3)

Plugged In Jock

Dirty White Guys

HOME ON THE RANGE

there are
two little girls
rolling towards me
in wheelchairs

one is extremely fat
and barely fits in her chair
the other is younger
smaller
and smoking cigarettes

i can smell her from here
and she stinks

they're yelling at me
what sounds
like antisemitic slurs
but as they get closer
i realize
it's just lyrics
to a Taylor Swift song
i used to hear
my brother sing
in the car ride to school

they finally approach
and ask
if i want to
pet their Alpacas

i didn't
but i said
yes anyways

they took me by the hand
and wheeled me around
to the back

their mom came out
also in a wheelchair
and asked if
i would be willing
to pay them
to see the Alpacas
and offered to let me
milk one of them
if i paid extra

i had no interest
in seeing or milking
anything

i also had no money
and told them this

all three instantly
became enraged
and started yelling
antisemitic slurs at me

they told me
the only good Jew
they ever met
was in a Walmart
candle aisle
and they only liked him
because he dropped
a $50 bill
and didn't realize it

EVERYTHING A GIRL I LIKE DID IN BED AT TWENTY-THREE

Took phone calls

Applied for jobs

Watched YouTube

Wrote a novel

Painted her nails

Cuddled her stuffed animals

Daydreamed about being interviewed
on late night television

Worried about the possibility
of her hair falling out

Got overheated (in the summer)

Touched herself

Ate lunch

Ate dinner

Slept

Cried

and called me

PINK

pink
is the color of my sheets
four weeks
after we last had sex
and i still haven't
washed them

MARGE

in 5th grade
i used to pay
my friend
$5 to draw
Marge Simpson naked

he'd charge me extra
to do it in color
but it was
worth the money

i'd take the drawings
to the bathroom after
and touch myself
in between classes

i used them so much
i had to get a plastic sheet
to protect them

my friend and i
eventually lost touch
and i found out
a few years ago
that he overdosed
and died

i still have the drawings though
still in the plastic sheets
and still touch myself
to them sometimes

THE SUPER MAN

i wish
i could
have an orgy
with myself

MASTERS OF THE UNIVERSE

Fidel Castro slept with 35,000 women

Wilt Chamberlain slept with 20,000 women

Warren Beatty slept with around 12,775 women

Ric Flair slept with over 10,000 women

Charlie Sheen slept with over 5,000 women

Gene Simmons slept with almost 4,800 women

Mick Jagger slept with at least 4,000 people

John Oates slept with "thousands"

Lamar Odom slept with over 2,000 women

Dustin Diamond slept with over 2,000 women

Keith Richards slept with 2,000 people

Simon Cowell slept with 2,000 women

Dennis Rodman slept with 2,000 women

Hugh Hefner slept with over 1,000 women

Russell Brand slept with over 1,000 women

Jennifer Coolidge slept with over 200 people

Lindsay Lohan slept with 36 men

Amy Schumer slept with 28 men

Mariah Carey slept with 5 people

and no one cares
how many people
i've slept with

MOM

my mom did porn
and sometimes
when i miss her
i watch her videos

OFF COURSE

boys are bulimic
and girls are
lifting weights

A RIVER RUNS THROUGH IT

we had a romantic evening

a bottle of wine
fettuccini alfredo
and now we're on
the subway home

there's no one else
on the train
so we touch
and kiss a little

but i can feel the wine
start to unravel
and filter through me

i told you
i might have to get off
to find a bathroom

you eagerly suggested

just do it on the train
right into your pants
we can do it together
lets see what happens

i hadn't done that before
but you said it
with such conviction
that it made it feel
like it was ok

i went first
it felt so unnatural
trying to push the pee out
with my pants
still wrapped around my legs

at first
only little droplets
sprinkled out

i could see it
start to
stain through
my beige khakis

i pushed harder
letting go of the hold
letting go of everything
i'd been trained not to do

and just letting it pour out
into my pants
down my leg
and onto the floor

it felt amazing
it felt like
running through a sprinkler
as a kid

the pee
ricocheting off my pants
and all over me

it looked like gatorade
staining the floors of the train

i looked over
and you were smiling
so i pushed harder

and then you
with your pale rosy thighs
wrapped
in your little plaid skirt
let it spray out
all over your legs
all over
the orange subway seats

it looked like
a waterfall screensaver
as it slowly
dripped over
the edge of the seats
onto the floor

our pee puddles
slowly merged together
and we watched it
trickle down
to the other side
of the train

conjoined
congealed
and connected

TRUE LOVE

you performed
Annie Get Your Gun
in full
for me
in bed

GETTING SPANKED AT TARGET

spank me
right now
not in the fitting room you pussy
right here by the blenders
blend me baby
do it hard
make it slap
make it clap
i wanna hear it whack
i want the kids in the fitting rooms
across the store to hear it
grab a spatula
and beat me like an egg
scramble me
crack me open
in the middle of Target
flip me on a bean bag
and make my ass wag
get me a Frappuccino from the front
or a glass of vino from the back
let it soak in
let 'em close
i ain't leavin'
then off with the lights
we've got our own
now get in the zone
and go get a racquet
and whack it
against my ass
and don't let a second pass
where i'm not as red
as a target

LIFE CYCLE

she said
she wanted to
consume me

she wanted us to
become one

to be as close
as possible

closer
than any other lover
either of us
has ever had

i didn't understand
what she was implying
or what else
we could do
to become that close

weeks went by
and nothing changed

we were close
but not one yet

months went by
and then one day
i came home
from work
and she was
sticking a carrot
inside of her vagina

she barely
noticed me
walk in

she was rapidly
pushing it
in and out
until finally
after a few minutes
she called me over
and told me to
take a bite

i did what she said
and took a nibble
of the tip

when i finished
chewing
she put her hand
on my face and said

while you eat this carrot
think of every step
in the process
of how it got here
start with the seed
then the dirt
the sunshine
the water
the farmer
the trucks
the supermarket
and now
to the inside of my vagina
and into your mouth

and soon into your stomach
and then finally
we will be one

so i did what she said
i closed my eyes
and thought of every step

the earth
the dirt
the rain
the sun
the farmer
the truck
the supermarket
her vagina
my mouth
and my stomach

i opened my eyes
and took another bite

and all it made me feel
was a little hungrier

GALAXY QUEST

i sucked Madeline's P
while she licked Ella's V

and David put his P
in Zack's A
while Zack rubbed his P

i turned around
and sucked on
David's P
while Ella licked my A

the room is cold

Marianne and Elizabeth
crawled over to me
rubbed my P
and massaged my A

it's hard to concentrate

i put my F's in them
at the same time

Jeremy was on his
hands and knees
while Pete and Thomas
put their P's
in each of his hands

Brittany was in the shower
on her knees
sucking Justin's P
while he peed

Molly was in the corner
getting her N's sucked
by Alex
while she
rubbed her C

Rachel and Leigh
were taking turns
L'ing one another

Sophia was on her stomach
in the middle
of the room
while Russell
F'd her V
with his middle F
while she S'd
his P at the same time

everyone stopped to watch

he grabbed her A
while she
continued to suck his P

he turned her over
got on his knees
and licked her V
first on the outside
then made his way
deeper inside

Brittany came over
and sat on Sophia's F

Sophia grabbed Brittany's A
and pulled her closer

Russell continued touching his P
until he C'd

then Sophia C'd
on Brittany's F

David came over
got on top of Brittany
and he put his P
in her M
and they L'd and S'd
until they both C'd

everyone was
empty of C
covered
in C

and now ready
to go to sleep

ACKNOWLEDGMENTS

MOUTHFUL is for Mackenzie Thomas. You're the foundation of this book. Everything about you inspires me. Thank you for listening to me read countless hours worth of poems over the past few years. You pushed me to write a little hornier, a little sweeter, a little louder, and most importantly, to write unapologetically like myself. This would be a very different book without you.

Thank you to my family—Mom, Dad, Adam, and Hershey. I am what I am, and that's all that I am because of all of your love and support. Thank you for always letting me be me, even when that was embarrassing for all of us at times (especially the time I wore a beige velour jumpsuit to my Bar Mitzvah party).

I am sooo grateful to my editor Elinor Hitt. I still can't believe a Harvard PhD candidate edited this book. Thank you for saying "yes" years ago based on little more than our shared love of Sex and The City, The Bachelor, and romcoms. You have been a teacher, a friend, and a mentor throughout this process. Thank you for helping me give life to this little monster. Thank you to my Dream Baby Press partner Zack Roif. It's been a wild ride and I couldn't have done it without you.

A special thank you to Larry Charles and Brontez Purnell for making the type of art that gives me the confidence to make mine. You both inspire me in a million different ways.

Thank you to Olivia Aylmer, who has supported and inspired me from the very beginning. Even before I planned on writing a book, you knew exactly what to say to put gas in the tank. I'm lucky to have someone like you to help me understand myself better. A huge thank you to Jess Kuronen for helping me get this book past the finish line (while eating lots of hummus and getting distracted by erotica covers on the shelves at Left Bank Books). Thank you, thank you, thank you Julia Muell! You saved me and this book.

A MASSIVE THANK YOU TO ALL MY FRIENDS for inspiration during crucial moments, long conversations, edits, suggestions, long phone calls, listening to me read my poems, reading my poems, your patience, and most of all your support: Ronald Wohlman, Justin Wolverton, Roi Cydulkin, Steven Grimler, Mark Gorton, Addy Gorton, Samara Gorton, Jon Burgerman, Max Bartick, Adam Himebauch, Elmo, Daphné Jouanneteau, Lisa Ben-Hur, Willie Crane, Sara Boccaccini Meadows, Leigh Altshuler, Costa Damaskos, Sophia Anne Caruso, Sophie Browning, Anna Kodé, Amy Rose Spiegel, Alessandra Schade, Sophia June, Adam Dressner, Meka Boyle, Kyle Depew and Jon Vickers.

And finally—my entire heart and gratitude for Harry B. Miller: a guiding light. You are always with me.

Printed in the USA
CPSIA information can be obtained
at www.ICGtesting.com
LVHW072324041124
795692LV00031B/130